SURVIVING ASSAULT
Words that Rock & Quiet & Tell the Truth

SURVIVING ASSAULT

Words that Rock & Quiet & Tell the Truth

RESOURCE FOR THE LIVING

Diana Tokaji

Copyright 2019 by Diana Tokaji
All rights reserved.

ISBN 978-1-7341485-0-3

First Edition, 2019

Cover photo by Devi S. Laskar
Illustrations by Thien-Kim Pham
Book design by C'est Beau Designs

To
R.C. and A.H.

... power rises
running like hot blood
from the same source
as your pain.

—Audre Lorde

CONTENTS

To You, the Reader / 1
How to Use this Book / 3

Conversation 1: **PROTECT AGAINST NEGATIVITY** / 5
What is a Mudra? / 13
Mudra #1 · Svasti Mudra / 16

Conversation 2: **BELIEVE** / 21
Mudra #2 · Samputa Mudra / 32

Conversation 3: **MEANINGFUL ACTION** / 37
Mudra #3 · Matangi Mudra / 48

Conversation 4: **CREATE COURAGE** / 53
Mudra #4 · Ganesha Mudra / 70

Final Love Notes / 75
Resources / 79
Poem: O. Deletron & the Blue-Black Knowing After / 81

TO YOU, THE READER

The first writing must be gentle
and not even on computer.

Waves of sleep wish to crash over me, drowning the project,
fogging over the writing as it tries to emerge, but

> *Gentle*. If we are gentle the
> right words will un-submerge
> and emerge.

There are so many elements that go into surviving and re-aliving
after an assault. This is one of them. You reading this;
YOU finding this; you with me sharing this. This is
Meaningful Action...Connecting,
in ways that matter, ways that
go to the heart and also to the
feet — taking us somewhere, a
next step; a feeling of not being
alone; a march, a shout, any creative
way forward that is needed
in this moment.
It is not easy, but it is
meaningful action for me to write this,
and I thank you.

HOW TO USE THIS BOOK.

This book is for the reader to use exactly as she wishes.
It is intended to be a conversation, from one who's been through an assault and survived, to another who might be seeking and wondering how she'll survive.

It is not intended to be a how-to book. Because I can't imagine telling anyone the right way to survive.
It is intended to suggest ways to *rally the energy it takes to survive an assault.* Ways to be with oneself at moments of sinking. Ways to live on to the next moment. And resources within ourselves that may help us survive day by day by day by day by day.

The path, of course, is for each of us to find.
But that doesn't mean we have to be alone.
We walk this path together. Some of us have been this path.
Knowing that, and reminding ourselves of that truth, helps bolster us onward & actively forward, or inward toward quiet.

Along the way we might need to STOMP.
We might QUIVER.

We might shake and sob in our own arms; we might rock the hardship back and forth and spew it to the wind. We might dance or kick-box; we might organize our whole city to change a law. We might slice apples and peaches and pit cherries to make a pie and see it whole and good and done.

No one can tell us the right way to survive this moment and the next.
But we know. When we connect to the gem within, to our wisdom, to our knowledge, we know. *Even now* we know how to survive this moment.

We might feel we've climbed eight mountains and swam an ocean *just to rise in the morning*. But we do know how…we do know how to guide ourselves.

May this speak to you.
May it help muster strength, or solace.
May it remind you that we are here, we who've walked this path and struggled and failed and lived.

No, it is not a how-to book. It is a conversation with you from the depth of my being, illuminating through words that rock and quiet and tell the truth, how to pull from the stars and the ether and the people and the ground, a way forward now, to your good life.

CONVERSATION 1

Conversation 1
PROTECT AGAINST NEGATIVITY

"Stay with the allies."
Cousin Jane wrote this to me at a time when I thought I might go mad. It is an odd and painful phenomenon that at a time of such heightened need, some friends and some family won't show up. They won't be helpful, they won't defend us, they might not even believe.

When my cousin wrote *stay with the allies*,
it was via the cold communication of an email,
but it went directly to my heart

    and it spoke clearly to my brain:
        some of these people are not your friends at this step — this is real.

        If they are damaging our focus on survival, we look elsewhere. Notice the friend who showed up out of the woodwork. Notice the family member

>who brought us food. Notice the tree
>whose beauty speaks as if purposely to
>us. Notice the pet whose presence
>helps. Notice the photo of an
>ancestor whose wisdom still supports.

Re-focusing on the allies will allow those who can't get it together, time to figure themselves out.
They might never come around — for some reason assault might just be beyond their scope of empathy.

>We cannot expend energy convincing them,
>or re-telling what happened — yet again —
>with hope that they will "get it."

But wait! I was a victim of this, we might want to shout.
I was hurt by it.

Scenarios might run through our head and we might brainstorm on ways to make folks care.
Just know this:

>*some people will not be there right now, no matter what we do.*

Others will "get it" gradually —
because of something we say
or something they see
that brings a clearer picture.

And some people — some we never expected, and some we knew would try —
will be our allies.

They might not pave the path to recovery for us, they might not *do* anything,
but when we imagine or make a list of our allies, these people will come up.
Like a soccer team with lead players and substitute players, they'll have
different positions on the field or the bench, active or passive at different times.

But just conjuring them up in our mind will sometimes be enough to get by…
and to get stronger, with one more day, and another and another.

Who are our allies?
    Those who sit beside us without judgment.
        Those who are able to listen.
            Those who can be helpful on our behalf.
                Those who show care through actions little or huge.
                    Those whose presence or whose eyes communicate kindness,
                      or supportive rage at what has happened.

STAY WITH THE ALLIES. PROTECT AGAINST NEGATIVITY.

This is all true…but wait!

In the meantime,
Something that shouldn't have happened
      — that in a fair and just world should not have happened —
has happened.

We protect our bodies against more harm.
We 'stay with the allies' to ensure that.
We stand by ourselves now, at our most needed time.
We let ourselves know this over and over again.
We protect ourselves against further negativity of any kind.
Even against negative voices of self-blame or shame.

Here is a mudra — Svasti Mudra — that was ever so helpful to me when negativity came at me, whether from another person, or from within myself.

When I found it — I was in a bookstore and picked up a book on mudras — it jumped off the page and it was like a friend exploded into my damaged life. I've used it often since. It strengthens me low in the belly, deep in my back.

But first, *what is a mudra?*

MUDRA
A Tool for Life

What is a mudra?
A gesture or "seal" in ritual dance and ancient practices
that can affect or "seal in" specific energy.

Mudras are ancient hand gestures
from Hinduism and Buddhism.
They create a focal point.
They may support us at great time of need.
They may shift our thoughts, our energy, our muscle tone,
our breath.
They can be done sitting, standing, in a yoga pose,
and *anywhere* we are.

Mudras can activate sensation in a positive, powerful way.
This might include a connected feeling, a strengthened feeling, a softening, or a surfacing of emotion.
Trust the safety of our own presence, or of another who is present.
Allow.
Speak or write or move or be still and notice.
Give permission to tears, shaking, words, sounds, shapes, movements, declarations, realizations, or quiet.
When closing, we can offer gratitude to our self for our presence to the truth.
We might end with this simple gesture of hands connected to heart,
or choose a gesture of our own to close.

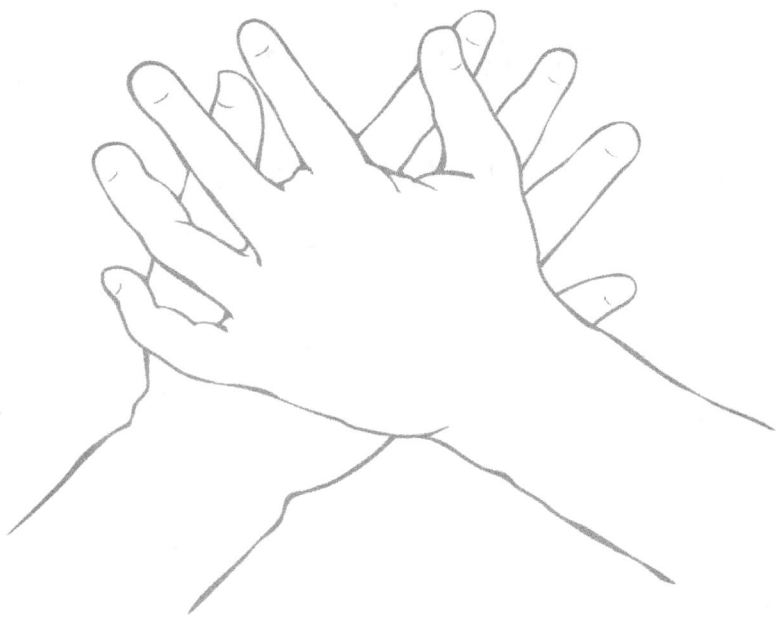

You will find one mudra corresponding to each conversation in this book. There are many other mudra, but I've chosen these four for us because they supported me greatly and I wish to share them. The hands to heart mudra above can be used anytime to return to self-nurturance, including after you've held one of the other selected mudras for a few breaths or longer.

Now let's learn our first thematic and powerful mudra, Svasti, protection against negativity.

Mudra #1

SVASTI MUDRA

Protection Against Negativity

How: Cross right and left forearms in front of chest, with the left on the outside.
Flex wrists as if closed fingers and palms stop negativity from the sides.
Press forearms isometrically into each other as if to stop negativity from the front, and notice awakened back muscles while doing this, as if to stop negativity behind.
Notice a rooting, toning sensation low in belly, all the way to feet and seat.
Receive strength and power; be kind/loving to self as sensations or emotions arise.

When: As a focused practice recalling a time when we weren't protected from negativity.
As an action when powerlessness surfaces.
As a choice when we feel a trigger coming on, especially when from negativity.
In private (car, bathroom) when negative words or actions have been thrown at us.
To catch, stop, and shift our own negative inner dialogue.
When external energies or circumstances make us feel defeated.
With Svasti Mudra, we feel power arising, supporting us now and forward.

This page is open for thoughts, drawings, words, ideas, needs, actions, wishes, prayers.

CONVERSATION 2

Conversation 2
BELIEVE

This section is about light.
Assault — whatever form it is —
is a blast of darkness
and it may threaten to douse our light.

It musn't.

If we have not yet called up all our forces of
      strength, courage, positive rage, passion, power, and commitment,

    we call them up now. Because:

    belief in our wisdom
    &
    belief in our ability to prevail

…these are the life rafts to a body
alone at sea in danger of
drowning. **Hold onto Belief.**
We hold onto belief
with all the Vigor we have left
& with
discipline
we keep holding.

Please take this in:
With *discipline* keep holding.

There will be letting go moments.
Fine. It's okay.

Sob, tantrum; we hold ourselves
lovingly through despair.

But we keep the raft in sight.
Touch it.
Hold it again.
Climb on & rest.
Bathe in the light of knowing it's there.

                    Light is critical.
                    Climb on to the raft!

There are 82 zillion ways the
Dark will try to overcome us.
      See it.
There will be trickery;
      sneaky, defiling, shame-blame ways — old & new —
      to take us down.

Imagine an injured cat.
Or an injured fish

      & how that open wound makes
      them prey to further attack…

After an assault we are so

      very vulnerable.
      Every kindness is noticed.
      Every not bad moment is a gift
      and every self-harming action
      or self-harming word

    or

        self-harming thought

            punishes us further.

                We are Beloved.
                We are Here for a reason.
                We are our most precious being.
                And we are Agent to that being.

That means:

we must be our *own* ally.

now more than ever.

    As we walk through the darkness

    we speak kindly to ourselves.

            We draw in LIGHT.

How do we do that?

    It takes time to gather enough light
    to overpower dark events, but
    we gather, we begin now, & every
    droplet & ray of light, brightens
    the body, making us stronger to fight.

    It is a battle some days to fight
    the amount, the degree, the LEVEL
    of darkness that has hit us.

Some days, KICK BACK
Some days, SHOUT NO
Some days, Haul & Vomit & Cleanse from horror

  & then pause.

      Pause so we might
      Draw Light
      into our vessel

      in every & any
      way we know.

         This is *Essential*.

Grocery list of things that feed us with light. Please add your own.

Food that feels godsent —

Liquid that is nectar to our throat —

The light of beauty —

        Nature — a rock, water, a branch surrounded by sky

        Art — music, movement, writing, a photo or painting

        Tiny Things — a smooth made bed, our hands on a pet, sip of tea

The presence of another —

        animal or human

        who breeds light

The remembrance of another —

        a being or angel or ancestor

        who breeds light

        who speaks to us with love

Our own wisdom —

        beyond the dark & terror & pain

        to the deepest well of

        knowing:

        We receive our own wisdom here

Prayer — in the form of
                writing
                singing
                whispering
                or speaking — loud enough for spirit to hear

        call, ask, beg

                for what we want
                and for
                      what we need
                          to live.

And if a wise book or a cartoon book or a seasonal TV show pulls us in and lets us rest, Read it. Watch it.

If it feeds us. If it breeds more light.

I followed LaPorsha Renae on American Idol, and her voice of glory sang right to my hollow place.
She had been a victim of domestic violence, had lived in a shelter with her baby, and was now singing for her life. Her courage and talent and abundance filled me with belief: it was a deliverance.

                Insist on Belief.

BELIEVE. FEED BELIEF WITH LIGHT.

Mudra #2

SAMPUTA MUDRA

Gesture of the Treasure Chest

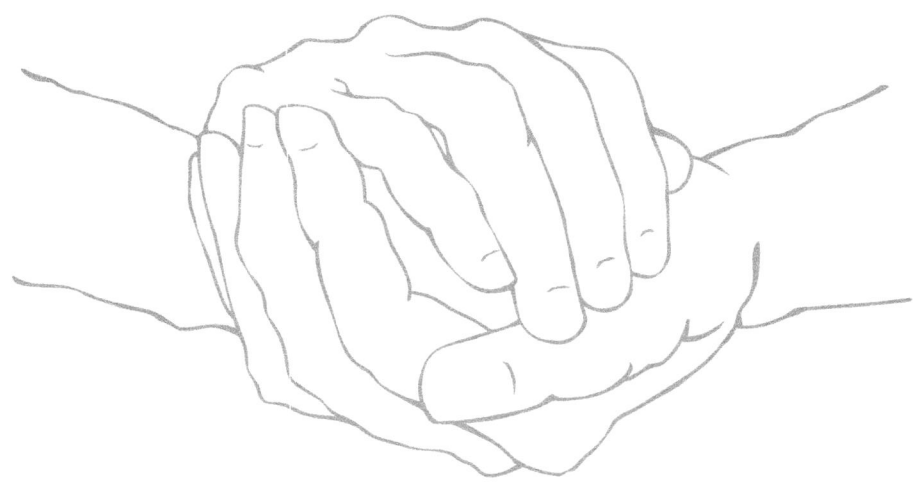

How: Cup right hand atop left cupped hand, forming the "treasure chest."

Rest this at a natural height that is comfortable, for example near the belly.

Invite shoulders, back, and elbows to relax.

We focus on what we know to be true. The truth is cupped in our hands.

If this surfaces an emotional response, remain loving and listen well.

We focus on our belief in our knowing. And our belief in our self.

We might imagine what we cup in the "treasure chest"

— a radiant gem, or light, our story, or our valued spirit.

When: When people have challenged what we think to be true.

If we've begun to doubt our knowing and our own capability.

If feeling "shattered" or raw, to gently engulf our spirit in protective hands.

If overpowering forces have disrupted our body/soul and we must collect toward a midline.

Here, in our cupped hands we return to a true and reliable source, our center.

We know our truth.

This page is open for thoughts, drawings, words, ideas, needs, actions, wishes, prayers.

CONVERSATION 3

Conversation 3

MEANINGFUL ACTION

Five years since I was assaulted, I am writing this book to you: *meaningful action*.

It is meaningful to me and meaningful to you.
It requires single focus, discipline, skill, passion.

But...

What do I mean by Meaningful Action?

I mean anything that serves us personally, supports us, elevates us.
I mean anything that serves others, supports others, elevates others.

Is a poem meaningful action?   YES
Is a protest meaningful action?   YES

Is a haircut or a bath with rose oil meaningful action?   YES

Is care of another animal or person or plant meaningful action?   YES
Even our hand on another's shoulder might be remembered, might strengthen.

Is documenting what happened meaningful action?   YES!
Is speaking our truth?   Oh, YES YES YES

How about singing?
        drawing?
                making a collage of random scraps to express base feelings
                      we cannot speak?

And time with our body…

…time to let our body express —

                moving, dancing, walking
           laying our own hands kindly upon our own body,
              wearing a fabric that comforts,
                a color that elevates,

punching a punching bag,
pulling a rope, planting a tree, lifting weights,
kicking, jumping, swimming,
rock-climbing, pressing heels or palms firm to the earth
or against a wall, or palms firm to desk, table, countertop
connecting firmly to the ground or to grounded objects.

how about cleaning? washing?
scrubbing a tub, chopping carrots and potatoes for soup,
making a bed with fresh sheets?
these are productive tasks that say, I LIVE.

and how about shoveling, knitting, hammering,

lifting furniture, folding laundry with a friend or with the radio on —
because: mindless tasks allow our brains to relax and

Process
process what is so difficult to process;
what is so difficult to *digest*.

We give our minds *safe rests* which result in
productive accomplishment,
completing something small,
feeling victorious
over something
as simple as
re-planting a plant.

These steps matter.

Martial arts are grounding.
African Dance is expressive, grounding, rhythmic.
Baseball, tennis, soccer… allow us to make contact with an object.
Zumba, yoga…we do the activity that our body says yes to. But if our usual activity distresses us now,
please know this is normal.

Be kind.
And be smart.

Listen.
Our body might not respond positively to its usual activity...

    We can do a *different* version of our old activity for now,
    or turn sideways and pick up something new.

AND if we're compelled in time for
bigger Actions...

Lead the Way
Speak Out

YOUR MOST COURAGEOUS VOICE MATTERS.

And if for now
it is challenge enough
to be able to close our eyes at night
and love our self in the morning
this is Meaningful Action.

Some Meaningful Actions that helped me:

Filing a citizen's complaint
Testifying before the State House of Representatives
Writing books, essays, poems
Cleaning the kitchen and bathroom
Marching with women against police violence
Training professionals to support assault survivors
Pulling weeds and invasive vines that were choking flowers
Creating a performance as a fundraiser to write this
Guiding my family out of shame

Some of the physical activities that helped me:

Boxing — to hit angrily and hard without harming (I'd never boxed)
Swimming — to cool my inflamed, swollen skin (I am not a swimmer)
Walking — under my favorite trees who I spoke to
Dancing — angry dances alone in the kitchen with Olatunji drums.
Zumba — sometimes they had free Zumba in an outdoor plaza near me, and I would dance with women of all ages and sizes I had never met.
Yoga — but for the first year I did not do relaxing yoga.

I did grounding poses with my eyes open.

    Read that again:

           I did grounding poses with my eyes open.

    One more time:

           Grounded. Eyes Open.

EACH MEANINGFUL ACTION ELEVATES OUR SPIRIT.

Mudra #3
MATANGI MUDRA

Gesture of the Goddess of Transformation

How: Interlace fingers together, right thumb in front.

Release third fingers and firm them together.

Center the wrists in the area of the solar plexus, near the lower ribs.

Point third fingers down, out, or up, a personal choice.

Relax shoulders and arms, then either remain still and quiet in the gesture

or allow the third fingers to lead a path in the air.

When: If we lack confidence or direction; if energy is lethargic or oppressed.

If we need to digest what happened and listen deeply within, in order to transform.

To regroup at the solar plexus, center of the sun and personal power.

To clear our path, to see our path, or to align our path in the world.

Matangi symbolizes wisdom to penetrate through false boundaries.

She is the Hindu Goddess of the spoken word and transformation of energy.

Use this mudra to listen, to manifest speech, music, dance, and knowledge.

This page is open for thoughts, drawings, words, ideas, needs, actions, wishes, prayers.

CONVERSATION 4

Conversation 4
CREATE COURAGE.

Watch out for *I can't*.
Watch out for *I don't have the strength*.

We often "don't have what it takes" to survive an assault that has hit our

        hearts
          our
        beliefs
          our
        morals
          our
        bodies
          our
        dreams.

        It is true. It is totally possible.

And yes, (oh such sadness to state the truth but), yes,
sometimes we are taken down.

We cannot fight 24/7.
No one can live on a battlefield
by day & by night forever.

    We might need to rally

HUGE HELP

    We might need to quit some of life as we had pictured it.
    We might need to
        get away for awhile
                or forever
We might need to
    fight   — the system
        — another person
We might need to
    fight for — our rights
        — our body's health
        — our family
        — our safety.

How is this possible

when we have been harmed and are in our most vulnerable state?

We might need massive support to do all this.

To write this book I have had to

Raise funds

Go to another country

Feel safe in this environment

& even then I had to

> Not use the computer.
> Write in long hand with my favorite pen.
> Stop to eat at intervals
> (strengthening, light food so I can think clearly).
> Stop for soothing, invigorating tea at intervals
> (for me green tea with fresh lemon).
> Do strengthening yoga poses before writing and at intervals.
> Collect rocks by the water and place them around me as I write.
> Hear loud but safe sounds of the pizzeria cooking and clambering as they wash pots & pans in the sink across the patio.
> Set up a fan to cool me from the heat, and also because this is work that takes me back to inflamed sensation.

IT HAS BEEN FIVE YEARS
And much of it was hell.

I can still be triggered.
I still do not go out alone at night.
I can still feel the cops on my back.
My knees, especially my left, still hurt.
I still shake.

I survived on WISDOM.
I relied on CREATIVITY.

I believed in
                my human step-by-step
                trudging-through-mud-&-sludge
                path…

            my divine
              path.

By "Creativity" do I mean that

      I can paint a picture & magically heal?

No. Although that could be a path.

What I mean is this:
      When we are in the big heat of
      Life where we are up against
      Intense energies that can
            Penetrate with
      Evil
      &
      Darkness
      &
      Malicious intent

We not only must *draw in light*
      draw upon belief
      draw on our wisdom

      but we must
      Be More Creative Than Ever Before

Again, what do I mean by that?
I have been hesitating to share personal story here, but I will cave.

*I was experiencing thoughts about suicide
when I came up with one of my most
creative actions, which helped me
through one more very tough month.
It was a time when I felt that*
      No One Believed Me,
a poisonous recipe for despair.

In short,
*When the director of a homeless shelter, where I went to offer required community service, refused my service saying that if I'd assaulted an officer I could not work there, this final slap did me in. My case had been "expunged" because the accusation was false, but he didn't care. I wept convulsing sobs as I walked home in a pelting, cold rain. This felt like the path to insanity, starting with being assaulted, arrested, and framed by the police; leading down a slippery slope where an assault can lead to being fired from a job or being unwelcomed at a job, being unable to pay the rent, marriage problems, kids in the mix, homelessness, mental stability slipping lower with each mean act. Until I could lose ground altogether.
I no longer wished to live in this world.*

I feel despair freshly as I write — no wonder I didn't want to share this. But we must share that it is not lilies afloat in a pond, it is not even "the lotus flower at home in muddy water," it is sometimes like sinking sand with no visible way out. ***If darkness penetrates our sanctity, we might wish to disappear.***

But this is not CREATIVITY.
This is despondence.
This is the victory lap of darkness
    when it prevails and takes us down.

This is when we dig —
        deeper than we've ever dug —
        for RESOURCE.

We must be Creative.
The oddest message may come.

LISTEN.
Within it is wisdom.

It will be colorful. It will be unexpected.
It will be unusual. It will be ours
      and only ours.

It will be the path for that
    RESURGENCE
      that moment; that re-lit moment.
              Please remember this:
      I wanted to GIVE UP, never try again. Never speak up again.
          I wanted to Turn My Lights OUT.

I choked on sobs and vomited in the street in the pouring rain.
I was soaked. I didn't care. I didn't care if I lived or died. No one was fighting for me. No one cared.

              I heard: ***GO SILENT.***

            I heard: ***Tell What Happened. Silently.***

Four times on four cold winter nights, outside in the alley where I'd been assaulted,
I held a silent vigil.
By flashlight, I shared pages of my story with any neighbors and friends who chose to come by.
In the dark cold nights, I strung a roll of easel paper across our back fence where people could sign that they bore witness to my story of what happened.
In this way, I told them without speaking.

It sounds unpleasant, doesn't it — the rain and snow, the dark, standing outside for hours in this vigil? It was.
And I'd hoped that some action would come of it, though no immediate action did.

But listen well:
It was SURVIVAL to me then.
Why?
Because I'd reached a point where I had no voice. I was powerless.
Yet I found a way to "speak."
To write and silently tell people what had happened without weakening my own spirit.
This was power.

Later, continuing to feel unsafe,
the question would arise, *how can I continue to live here, in this house, this county, this country?*

I have had to write the truth about that corner of my yard where I was flattened and handcuffed.
And leave it.
I have had to think up Creative and Financially Clever Ways to *leave my home* for months of each year.
It is my health & sanity to both keep my home and leave my home.

I accept it as the place where the unforgettable happened.
& I take breaks from it
    so I can creatively heal.

       One step at a time.

This is a tiny bit of my path. It is not yours.
I can name countless other CREATIVE

exploits that helped me through dangerous potholes —
testifying on police reform; working with assault survivors; writing powerful
poems, essays, articles, and three books.
But do not be literal about these examples.

>One might write an opera
>One might change laws
>One might create an organization
>>that reduces suffering
>
>One might sit simply and quietly
>One might cook the most fragrant stew
>>for herself, for her family,
>>for the hungry.

Creativity is the hand of wisdom.
Creativity is the heart radiating.
Creativity is the weakened spirit calling light into real form.
Creativity is a rope ladder out of the darkest well.
Creativity is embodied design. It is the DOING of one unique step to redirect us on our path.

when no one else has the answer,
when no way seems a way out,
when we are stuck,
when we think we cannot survive,

      We dig deeper into Wisdom.
      We commit to Belief.

And we celebrate even the strangest hieroglyph we receive as a message.
      Our message!

This is Creativity,
Light in unique form just for us,
that directs us to yet brighter light.

IT REQUIRES ENACTMENT: *Action*

IT REQUIRES DISCIPLINE: *See it through.*

IT REQUIRES BELIEF: *Dare to be unusual. This moment calls for unusual choice.*

It calls for............. Voice.

> ➤ *Not stoicism.*
> ➤ *Not toughness*
> ➤ *the courage to cry*
>   *and love ourselves the whole time*

The courage to impale dark forces & doubts that come at us.
The courage to speak with our selves honestly & to listen
— even to what we don't want to hear.

The courage to be uncomfortable and still arise.
The courage to lift ourselves with love when we have no strength.

Yes, even now if we are experiencing despair:

the courage to follow our deepest wisdom and be willing to
KNOW what is real, true, what is next. And to creatively follow that truth.

CREATE COURAGE. TRUST DEEPEST WISDOM.

Mudra #4

GANESHA MUDRA

Strength to Overcome Obstacles

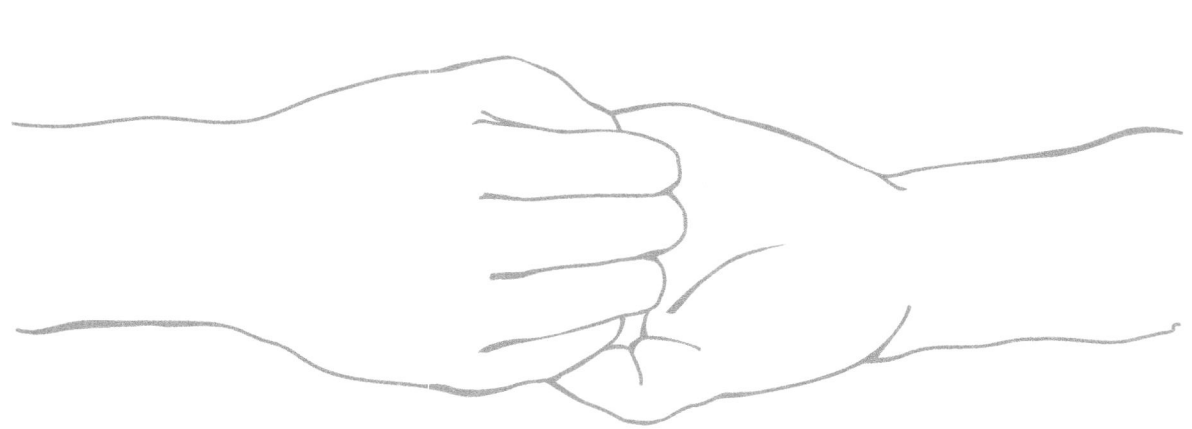

How: Bring palms together in a prayer position in front of the chest.

Swivel hands until fingertips point toward opposite elbows, right palm facing heart.

Fold fingers while sliding hands slightly away until right and left fingers interlock.

Pull on locked hands and sense how this creates vigor.

Release undue tension, yet notice strength arise in back muscles and navel center.

Hold for a pleasing length of time. Optionally switch hands (not necessary).

Pulse option: relax upon inhale, re-invigorate the pull upon exhale. Repeat.

Mudra hands can rest on the sternum, sensing broad width when pulling.

When: Ganesha tones shoulders, chest, back muscles, arms, abdomen, and pelvic floor,

hence it can motivate both our metabolism and our spirit into awakened action.

In this way, we can use it to breed courage.

If defeat or exhaustion prevail, Ganesha Mudra might stoke strength and inner fire.

It may help us organize our system to creatively overcome obstructions in our way.

This mudra is named for "the elephant god who removes all obstacles."

This page is open for thoughts, drawings, words, ideas, needs, actions, wishes, prayers.

FINAL LOVE NOTES

Is that it?
Gravel under the skin and I give out band aids?
Wave a wand and a good witch leads us down the path — and the path is jolly?

No, we are going to have to seek allies and stay with the allies.
If the ally is a tree, a dog, a smooth weighty rock in our palm, that is our ally.
If the ally is a whole community, or an extended family, or a nation,
that is our ally.
If our ally is a lit candle and a prayer to our grandma who we loved and loved us and was wise,

then candlelight and her memory and invoking the warmth of her eyes — this is our ally.

Negative powers are strong. They like to conglomerate. Once they latch on, it seems we'll never get them off.
They seem to attract more negativity and pretty soon it's a pile on.
On us. On our bodies and on our spirits.

It might be a wrestling match. A tough one.

We will need bystanders who root us on with devotional enthusiasm.

We will need water, food, and love for sustenance.

We will need to activate, integrate, and care for our bodies.

We will need safety.

We will need to choose creative and meaningful actions for our survival.

This can be done. With great will we can do this work — to survive.

And to re-alive.

And we can help it along — with music or written words that spur us on.
                                        with rests along the way.
                                        with love and belief in ourselves.

Gentle love to ourselves. YET: Strong;
                                                      Courageous;
                                                      Disciplined.

It is our *WILL* facing off against negativity.

We know how powerful negativity is.

Therefore, **we must ratchet up our WILL like never before** *to see ourselves through.*

Am I saying "Be Brave"?
NO.
I am saying CREATE A BREEDING GROUND FOR COURAGE.
We stoke courage, seek courage, and draw courage into our blood vessels.
What brings each of us courage will vary.
Whatever it is — and it might be many things and beings and actions —
    this is what we energize, this is who we spend time with, these are the actions we do.

I will end with a virtual embrace,
knowing we feel each other across these words,
knowing today we share this vicious, courageous, righteous fight for survival.

I could have written this book 66 different ways, and I tried many of them.
But in the end, I decided I don't need to explain to an assault survivor what an assault is.

I don't need to describe scientifically what an assault does to our nervous system, or how at first it is like a deep skin wound that is open to the elements.

I decided to talk together directly and speak to the bottom line.

I decided the bottom lines are what I've shared:

>Protect Against Negativity.

>Believe.

>Take Meaningful Action.

>Create Courage. Trust Wisdom.

And now, because it's hard to leave, even though I trust every one of us
to find our way…
I'll leave with a list of resources, a poem I wrote, and my love, faith, and all my being believing in us.

Always,
Diana

RESOURCES

This is a list of a few resources that made a difference in my survival.

1. **R.A.I.N. = Recognize, Allow, Investigate, Nurture.**
   A practice offered by Tara Brach in written or audio form.
   http://www.tarabrach.com/wp-content/uploads/pdf/RAIN-of-Self-Compassion2.pdf

   One of the best tools I used
   - To *understand* what was happening every day, every hour
   - To *listen well* to myself, which bred self-love
   - To *access wisdom* to handle difficult feelings, people, and circumstances.

2. **MUDRA**
   Many mudra books abound, and here are several.
   One can also use google to request mudra for what one seeks, for example:
   If I'm seeking to trust myself, I can google the words *mudra* and *trust*, and I'll find one of my favorites,
   Vajrapradama Mudra = Mudra for Unshakeable Trust
   I might look at more than one source that pops up because the same mudra can have several variations, and one might appeal to me more than another.

For books, three of my favorites are:

- *Mudras for Healing and Transformation* by Joseph and Lilian Le Page (book or stack of cards)
- *Mudras of India* by Cain and Revital Carroll
- *Mudras: Yoga in Your Hands* by Gertrud Hirschi

3. **YOGA THERAPY**

There are many wonderful forms of yoga therapy. The one that especially helped me was Phoenix Rising Yoga Therapy. I've been a certified practitioner of PRYT since 1997, so I was able to use some techniques with myself. The presence of a good Phoenix Rising Yoga Therapist is, well…to me, there's just nothing more supportive. Here's how to find a certified practitioner nearby: https://pryt.com/pryt-directory/

4. **WRITE TO ME**

To receive my article, or just to connect: dianatokaji@gmail.com

O. DELETRON & THE BLUE-BLACK KNOWING AFTER

I learn later, a squid,
octopoteuthis deletron,
though tiny, if attacked
or attacking can

grab its predator
with small suckers,
hook, dig, latch on
with pointed "teeth"

and self-
amputate, leaving
end pieces of its tentacles
in the predator's skin. O

Deletron, (The Clever),
breaks free, jettisons away
in a spray
of black ink, and foregoes

a piece of arm.
Attack autonomy
it's called. And I
want it. I want my

broken tips to flail for three
seconds, glow vigorously, my
light-producing organs
stuck on the outline

of attackers everywhere.
It was night.
In the waters that drowned me
it was pitch; I had no color.

But in the re-do,
I control
chromatophores.
And if I am only

five inches long, my
skin is the charged hue
of rage
and my tiny,

sucker-tipped tentacles
flash a revelatory
light show stuck hard
on those who dared.

And everyone knows
— everyone! —
as I, as we all,
swim free,

who I am,
who we tentacle-torn are,
and why O. inked
the blue sea.

ABOUT THE AUTHOR

DIANA TOKAJI, MSc, C-IAYT

Diana Tokaji is a writer, choreographer, and certified yoga therapist who specializes in a strength-focused approach following trauma. She has three other books forthcoming, including an essay collection, a poetry collection, and her nonfiction book, *Six Women in a Cell: Survival and Sisterhood After Police Assault.*

www.ingramcontent.com/pod-product-compliance
Lightning Source LLC
Chambersburg PA
CBHW051419070526
44584CB00023B/3500